THE BELONGING FACTOR

MOST ORGANIZATIONS have well-written and well-intentioned culture and values statements. They review them at big meetings and plaster them on the walls in the building. Designed to inform how the brand and the people behave, they are intended to have a positive impact on people, processes, and profits. The problem: A staggering majority of them are bullshit.

That said, there is a way to reimagine your values, your culture, and your brand in a way that inspires tremendous loyalty, builds community, and delivers profits. I am an award-winning sales leader, entrepreneur, and student of human behavior, and I can show you how.

The Belonging Factor is a system based on five characteristics shared by the most well-known brands and most successful leaders. It informs CEOs, executives, senior leaders, and anyone interested in building an authentic, inspired, and diverse culture, centered in a deep sense of belonging. In this book, I share stories of brands and leaders that are getting it done and those that aren't. The simple tools and practical application make *Belonging Factor* a must-have resource, no matter your title or position.

Whether you run your own company, coach a team, or have a passion for success because of people—not on the backs of them—*Belonging Factor* is the book you need to inspire teams, improve processes, and grow profits.

BE /
LONG
/ ING
FACTOR

How Great Brands and Great Leaders Inspire Loyalty,
Build Community, and Grow Profits

DEVIN R. HALLIDAY

PUBLISH
YOUR
PURPOSE®
PRESS

For permission requests, write to the publisher, addressed "Attention: Permissions Coordinator," at the address below.

Publish Your Purpose Press
141 Weston Street, #155
Hartford, CT, 06141

The opinions expressed by the Author are not necessarily those held by Publish Your Purpose Press.

Ordering Information: Quantity sales and special discounts are available on quantity purchases by corporations, associations, and others. For details, contact the publisher at orders@publishyourpurposepress.com.

Edited by: Katrin Jesswein & Karen Ang

Printed in the United States of America.
ISBN: 978-1-946384-80-5 (paperback)
ISBN: 978-1-946384-89-8 (hardcover)
ISBN: 978-1-946384-81-2 (ebook)
Library of Congress Control Number: In Progress

Second edition, September 2019.

The information contained within this book is strictly for informational purposes. The material may include information, products, or services by third parties. As such, the Author and Publisher do not assume responsibility or liability for any third-party material or opinions. The publisher is not responsible for websites (or their content) that are not owned by the publisher. Readers are advised to do their own due diligence when it comes to making decisions.

Publish Your Purpose Press works with authors, and aspiring authors, who have a story to tell and a brand to build. Do you have a book idea you would like us to consider publishing? Please visit PublishYourPurposePress.com for more information.

Disclaimer

The publisher and author make no representations or warranties concerning accuracy or completeness of the contents of this work, including, and without limitation, warranties of fitness for a particular purpose. No warranty may be created or suitable for every situation.

Nothing in this work is a promise or guarantee of earnings. The content, case studies, and examples shared in this work should not be assumed to represent in any way "average" or "typical" results. Neither the author nor the publisher is familiar with you, your business, your market, or your circumstances. Therefore, the case studies shared can neither represent nor guarantee the current or future experience of other past, current, or prospective clients. Rather, these case studies and examples represent what is possible by applying the strategies presented.

Each of these examples is the culmination of numerous factors, many of which we cannot control, including pricing, market conditions, product or service quality, offer, customer service, personal initiative, and countless other variables, tangible and intangible. Your level of success in attaining results is dependent on many factors, including your skill, knowledge, experience, ability, connections, dedication, focus, business savvy, and financial situation. Because these factors vary from individual to individual, we cannot guarantee your success or ability to earn revenue.

You alone are responsible for your actions and results in business and life, and in your use of these materials. You agree not to hold us liable for any of your decisions, activities, or results, at any time, or under any circumstances.

No portion of this work is intended to offer legal, medical, personal, or financial advice. If professional assistance is required, the services of a competent professional should be sought. Neither the publisher nor the author shall be liable for damages arising herefrom.

Under no circumstances, including but not limited to negligence, will the author or publisher, or any of their representatives or contractors be held liable for any special or consequential damages that result from the use of, or inability to use, the materials, information or success strategies communicated through this work, or any services following this work, even if advised of the possibility of such damages.

The fact that an organization, individual, or website is referred to as a source of further information does not mean that the author or publisher endorses the information the organization or website may provide or recommendations it may make. Further, readers should be aware that internet websites listed in this work may have changed or disappeared between when this work was written and when it was read.

In other words, nothing in this book should be taken as any form of contractual obligation. Neither the author, his company, the publishers, nor their assignees warrant any result from implementing the ideas in this book, and they accept no liability for any damage, loss, or harm to you or any third party arising from any interpretation or implementation of the ideas in this book.

For my dad, who taught me to believe in myself, and that anything is possible with the right attitude, preparation, and a little sweat.

Dear Reader,

I WANT to express my deepest gratitude to you for honoring yourself and your people with a commitment to building a sense of belonging at work. The fact that you are reading this book signifies a critical turning point in the future of those you are charged with looking after. Before plunging into the content, please indulge a few thoughts. To take this book as gospel and rely solely on the ideas and practices shared in the subsequent pages would fall short of the mark. The views in this book serve as a supplement to rather than replacement of the direction and guidance given by the seasoned diversity and inclusion professionals with whom you may already have a partnership.

The human condition is one filled with joyous wonder, unapologetic oddity, tremendous sorrow, and high aspiration. For all our differences, collectively, humans share a deep desire for connection, community, and a sense of belonging. Leaders of community and business understand that shared experience and collective belonging builds fulfillment and inspires loyalty.

This book is for those who choose to inspire, to lead, to fulfill, and to be fulfilled.

All the best,

CONTENTS

be·long

/bəˈlôNG/

verb

gerund or present participle: **belonging**

1. be a member or part of (a particular group, organization, or class).
   "they belong to garden and bridge clubs"
   synonyms: be a member of, be in, be included in, be affiliated to, be allied to, be associated with, be connected to, be linked to, be an adherent of
   "I don't belong to a labor union"

   - (of a person) fit in a specified place or environment.
     "she is a stranger, and doesn't belong here"
     synonyms: fit in, be suited to, have a rightful place, have a home, be part of; More
     antonyms: alienation

   - have the right personal or social qualities to be a member of a particular group.
     "young people are generally very anxious to belong"

2. (of a thing) be rightly placed in a specified position.
   "learning to place the blame where it belongs"

fac·tor

/ˈfaktər/

noun

noun: **factor**; plural noun: **factors**

1. a circumstance, fact, or influence that contributes to a result or outcome.
   "she worked fast, conscious of the time factor"
   synonyms: element, part, component, ingredient, strand, constituent, point, detail, item, feature, facet, aspect, characteristic, consideration, influence, circumstance, thing, determinant
   "this had been a key factor in his decision to withdraw"

2. a number or quantity that when multiplied with another produces a given number or expression.

   - MATHEMATICS

     a number or algebraic expression by which another is exactly divisible.

INTRODUCTION

A PRAGMATIC optimist. If such a person exists, I am that person. I choose to see wonder and splendor and the possibility of what can be, while squarely addressing what is right before me. I've found harmony in this dichotomy. It allows me to both validate the current circumstances and challenges, while understanding that they may change one day. This is what guides my why—to shape a world my children are proud of—and informs my how. My mission? To unlock and develop the potential in others to do more in the world. My what? To build community, culture, and belonging.

Do you want to create an organization so respected that your employees would have your company logo tattooed on their bodies? Have you ever desired to build a brand with such a secure connection that your customers are proud to emblazon it in their skin and show it off to the world? Admittedly, those might sound like strange questions. It's highly likely that these thoughts never crossed your mind when pondering your organization or brand. They should. There is something extraordinary that level of commitment says about the brand that every leader should aspire to build.

Harley-Davidson set out to build the best motorcycles in the world. Apple set out to create the best technology experience in the world. Ford and Chevy set out to produce durable, dependable automobiles. Amazon set out to revolutionize the way consumers buy products. While some may argue whether or not each has been successful in their intended endeavor, what can't be claimed is the sense of belonging each of those brands built with their customers, as evidenced by the millions of people who felt so connected, they committed the brand to their skin with a tattoo.

In this book, we will explore the value of belonging in the most rudimentary sense and its critical importance to both organizational development (internal) and brand experience (external). After all, not only is belonging a universal human need—it's a largely untapped business opportunity, as well.

Belonging Factor is divided into three parts, with the first outlining the critical need that belonging serves in society, and the impacts of the belonging deficit we are currently facing. This section takes a look back at our past to serve as a guide to inform our present and our future. It conveys the authentic story of a life filled with "things and stuff" (thank you, Sean Tyler), but lacking in belonging. After reading Part 1, you will better understand how a need to feel a sense of belonging shows up in life, and why it matters in the workplace and in a brand.

Part 2 is designed to help you understand the factors that must exist in the culture of an organization, a leader, or a brand to build a sense of belonging. This section also provides critical insights to help you prioritize the cultivation of that culture.

Understanding both of these perspectives will allow you to inspire any audience, no matter if they are champions of or resistant to workplace change. If you need more research to build your case for various audiences, you can locate all sources cited throughout this book in the Notes section located at the end of the book.

The third and final part of *Belonging Factor* provides the structure to build a culture of belonging, regardless of the level of leadership you currently serve in. This section details the practical steps to examine the existing culture within your organization and your brand. You are provided a set of actions you can implement in your everyday life to be a Belonging Factor master and a true champion of inclusion, diversity, and belonging. The last chapter of the book offers both coaching and access to a wealth of resources on how you can take the necessary steps to make the personal and organizational changes required to build belonging. It's exciting to get started, but it takes commitment and a plan to deliver the real impact.

As you read along, I encourage you to write in this book. Dog-ear pages, fill the margins, underline talking points that resonate with you, and use this book as a general roadmap to help your organization begin or enhance the journey of creating a deep sense of belonging.

You are invited to access the full digital toolkit that supports the activities discussed in this book. There, you will find worksheets, resource material, team meeting activities, and additional tools related to the book's content. This digital toolkit exists to help you digest and implement all that you will learn as you read through *Belonging Factor*. You should feel free to use these resources, with attribution to this book, to help educate your colleagues on important concepts featured throughout.

REGISTER YOUR BOOK TO ACCESS THE DIGITAL TOOLKIT

https://book.belongingfactor.com

Share your stories of how the Belonging Factor has helped you or your organization.

Tag us on social media:

#BelongingFactor

Connect, Like & Share:

Twitter: @BelongingFactor

Facebook: BelongingFactor

Instagram: BelongingFactor

LinkedIn: Devin Halliday

Podcast: podcast.belongingfactor.com

PART 1

A BELONGING DEFICIT

"There is a significant shift in the current culture that is opening up a void—a belonging deficit."

CHAPTER 1

How I Came to Believe in Belonging

"When we help ourselves, we find moments of happiness. When we help others, we find lasting fulfillment."

— *Simon Sinek*

AFTER MONTHS of avoiding the recruiter's calls and knocks at the door—I had just recently celebrated my eighteenth birthday—I did something out of character. I answered the phone, and when the caller identified himself as, "Bob, from the Navy office," I listened. I wrote down his number and agreed to call him back later that week. Although I was working at a restaurant and going to school full-time, I wasn't ready to be an independent adult just yet. However, somewhere in my heart, deep down, I knew I was going to join the Navy.

Bob couldn't have known that. He had no way of imagining that as a child I would wait in anticipation for October to roll around—that's when the Blue Angels, the U.S. Navy's flight demonstration squadron, always came to San Francisco for an airshow. He couldn't have dreamt that my favorite movie of all time was *Top Gun*—you know, the one where Maverick made a sport out of being a rebel and pissing off his commanding officers. Bob had no way to know that I held a deep respect for both of my grandfathers who served in the Navy during and after World War II.

Later that week, I called him—Bob, from the Navy office. After a brief ring, a voice barked out, "Petty Officer Scroggins, how may I help?" I identified myself and informed the voice that I was looking for Bob, and before I knew it, I was enlisted and off to Great Lakes, Illinois—the home of recruit training for the U.S. Navy. I wasn't going to fly planes, but I was going to be the person responsible for keeping them in the air. As a child, I used to envision myself belonging in high-performance aviation, and I was on my way to make that belief become a reality. I joined the Navy and became an airframe and hydraulics mechanic.

What I didn't necessarily understand was that to be part of that world also meant I had to be a shipmate, a sailor, and a mentally and physically disciplined young man. So, I learned how to be a shipmate, a sailor, and a mentally and physically disciplined young man—and I learned to be part of a team. In boot camp, I was taught how to remove selfish thoughts and prioritize the greater good—the mission. While it certainly wasn't as rough as the combat-focused training many brave service members faced, it brought about an understanding of the unique qualities we all have as individuals. What became immediately apparent in that environment was the need to learn to rely upon one another and have each other's back. Knowing that could mean life or death, there was no place for uniqueness, no opportunity to decide whether or not you want to belong or feel you should belong. It was merely about mission accomplishment, period. That was it.

Throughout my time in the Navy, I began to understand that my childhood idea of belonging was not entirely on the mark. The military certainly had a lot to offer to me—and I to it—but there was something else out there for me even though I fulfilled my dreams. I sailed around the world, lived in Japan, launched and recovered off the deck of my aircraft carrier, saw 23 countries, all while having my shipmates' backs. I proudly maintained the world's most elite aircraft and supported the pilots calling the cockpit their office.

There was a feeling of fulfillment, but what was lacking was a sense of long-term purpose.

As I left the military, I knew I needed to be in an environment where I could continue to find out who I was. Still very young, I was given an excellent opportunity to take a job with GTE Wireless, which merged with Bell Atlantic to form Verizon, shortly after I started. It was unfamiliar work—mobile phone installation and repair. I liked what I was learning and the people who surrounded me.

As time passed, I created several meaningful relationships, improved my abilities, and acquired new skills. I evolved into various roles, eventually accepting a general manager position. Somehow, I was now responsible for 32 people and $18M in revenue. I wasn't particularly good at leading people, and, as a result, my KPIs weren't stellar. I made many mistakes—I managed to the results, focused on numbers, and coached to output. I even emulated managers I despised, because I thought that was how the company expected its leaders to lead. Despite all that, I had it in my heart to listen to my people. I was bursting with curiosity about how they were feeling, collaborating, and achieving the goals they set. Before long, I had asked a ton of questions and solicited a myriad of ideas. I became fascinated by championing the ideas of others and building a team dynamic that produced happy people, fulfilled people—and I quickly learned: People matter more than any KPI.

In my mid-twenties, my worldview and my beliefs evolved to the point where I could start to feel that sense of purpose, fulfillment, and belonging I was chasing. It didn't only come from achieving my aspirations, but from helping others define and achieve theirs as well. I stopped limiting coaching solely to the achievement of performance goals and started collaborating with my people on how to achieve their life goals. I was no longer coaching to a metric but instead to what the people on my team wanted to accomplish. Jessica wanted to buy a house, then a boat, and, of course, a truck to tow the boat. Ross wanted financial independence to travel the world. Nate wanted to go to Burning Man and Coachella. DeAnna wanted to provide the best life for her daughter. Ruben and his wife wanted to start a family.

It was at this point that I saw the real impact this new philosophy had on KPIs and people's lives. By shifting my coaching focus to the people who were tasked to produce the results, all of us were able to interact more authentically and built a supportive and fulfilling community within that team. Oh, and we delivered benchmark results and received more than our fair share of accolades. I remember, as I was sitting at an awards dinner collecting trophies earned by the team that year, I couldn't help but reflect on how we got there. It was my *Field of Dreams* moment. The famous line from that movie was playing on repeat in my mind, "If you build it, they will come." Meaning, if you build a sense of belonging, success will follow.

I thought I had it all figured out. I realized what it took to win. I even replicated it on other teams I led in the following years. What I still didn't fully understand was why it worked so well.

I had the most humbling experience of my entire career—no, my life—when Verizon relocated me to the islands of Hawaii. It was there that I learned just how much I didn't know about connection, community, or how deep the sense of belonging is rooted within us. It took me about two months to see it. Once the luster of living in paradise started to fade, I began to take in what was happening around me. Whether it was the people who were charged into my care as a leader, or the people in the community at the grocery store, the beach, or the gas station, I began to take notice of something unfamiliar. I was hearing, seeing, and feeling Ohana.

In the Hawaiian language, *Ohana* means family. Only it means so much more than that. It extended to friends, coworkers, and community, and stands for a deep bond—a spiritual kind of love (Aloha). If you are out, you are out. However, if you are in, you are Ohana. Once I became aware of this cultural norm that felt so foreign to me, I became downright obsessed with learning why it was so ingrained in the Hawaiian people's culture. I took every opportunity to absorb every piece of information I could get, making a classroom out of everywhere. I found myself lingering even just a few minutes. From the silky sands of Lanikai to the crowded streets of Honolulu, I observed, I asked questions, and I gave myself and my energy to others.

What I took from these lessons was the answer to the question of why it is so critical to feeling a sense of belonging, and why that rightfully extends beyond your immediate loved ones. This is how I gained a transcendent level of understanding and learned how to create an environment where people really and genuinely feel they can be vulnerable and authentic—part of a community in which they want to belong.

"You tend to believe what you are taught and teach it to others."

CHAPTER 2

The Importance of Belonging

"No house should ever be on a hill or on anything. It should be of the hill. Belonging to it. Hill and house should live together each the happier for the other."

— *Frank Lloyd Wright*

TO UNDERSTAND why the sense of belonging is such an essential facet of the human condition, we need to take a closer look at what causes this strong desire within—a great deal of human behavior develops from a deeply rooted need to belong. At its core, belonging is the idea of being part of an environment that allows us to feel accepted within a social, religious, political, cultural, or socioeconomic group. It brings with it the feelings of security, inclusion, acceptance, relation, and conformity, which serves to enhance wellbeing.

When we feel accepted through the relationships and connections made with others and our need for belonging is satisfied, they begin to shape (or reshape) our identity. The question is, why is it that as humans, we tend to base so much of our character on how others experience or perceive us? Psychologist Christopher Peterson provides a simple explanation, "Other people matter, and we are all other people to everyone else."

Social acceptance matters so much that it can become a crucial factor in how we perceive our values. The qualities and characteristics we identify as uniquely our own begin to fade into the background of our identity as the connections we form with others grow. As we start to place more value in the groups where we feel a sense of belonging, we begin to redefine our identity, often blurring the lines between *I* (the individual) and *we* (the group).

Don't misjudge the importance of this behavioral pattern, however. Building identity based on connection and belonging is essential. It is as important a human need as food, water, and shelter. The feeling that "you belong" is one of the most critical emotions in seeing value in life itself. Some find belonging in a church, some with friends, some with family, some in a company, and many increasingly find it online—a majority of them on social media. Humanity has always been better served when connectedness and community build strength and support. A sense of belonging to a greater community improves motivation, health, and happiness.

In the context of organizational development, an employee's sense of belonging can be directly tied to their engagement, productivity, creativity, commitment, longevity, and impact. Universally, employees want to enjoy the work they are doing. They want to get along with their coworkers, and ultimately, they want to find meaning in their job.

I know, you may have cringed just a little when you were reading the word "engagement" above. I don't blame you. In the current business ethos, it has been used beyond its capacity and has even taken on a few new, very imaginative definitions. For the sake of context, let's agree that engagement means people enjoy their jobs, find value in their work, and like showing up every day.

Dr. Abraham Maslow, a well-known pioneer in the field of social psychology, championed his idea,

"Hierarchy of Needs," which ranks belonging as the third most important factor for personal satisfaction and fulfillment. To satisfy the need for social belonging in a work environment, an employee will look to build relationships with their coworkers. Even more ingrained in human nature, however, is the desire to connect with the vision and identity of their organization. Simply finding their work to be interesting isn't enough to spark a sense of organizational belonging. The mission of a leader should first and foremost be to build a clear, compelling vision and authentic identity, to foster an environment where employees feel part of the workplace because their work has meaning.

There is a significant shift in the current culture that is opening up a giant void—a belonging deficit. We live in a digital age, and increasingly see patterns once exclusively in an offline world emerging in and shaping a connected, online life. Digital disruption is on the rise. As attention spans continue to shorten, and our "always-on" brains keep being exposed to multiple screens, the bombardment of brand messages only serves to increase fragmentation.

Don't believe me? Check out these staggering statistics.

- **10,000:** Number of brand messages the average consumer is exposed to on a given day

- **8:** The average American attention span, in seconds

- **21:** Times per hour consumers switch between screens

- **40:** Percentage of 18-year-olds to 24-year-olds who say they've never felt an emotional connection to a brand or business.

From a behavioral standpoint, considering the fundamental human need to belong, this is dangerous. The superficial (artificial) connectivity experienced in the online world fosters a deceptive feeling of being connected yet alone, simply because connectedness does not correlate with belonging. It is possible to feel connected to people, brands, or ideas, but still not feel like you belong. It is a feeling that does not engender a sense of fulfillment or loyalty, both sentiments that can and will make a difference for competing businesses. Here's a number that should pique your interest:

- **55:** Percent of consumers who would pay more for a better customer experience

While it is vital that we acknowledge and consider the impact of technology on building brand belonging, that's not what the Belonging Factor is about. It is about people. Sebastian Junger, the famous war correspondent, may have best described this idea in his book, *Tribe*.

> *"We have a strong instinct to belong to small groups defined by clear purpose and understanding–tribes. This tribal connection has been largely lost in modern society, but regaining it may be the key to our psychological survival. Whatever the technological advances of modern society— and they are nearly miraculous—the individualized lifestyles those technologies spawn seem to be deeply brutalizing to the human spirit."*

A fully evolved brand understands that gaining followers on social media is not an accurate representation of brand loyalty. The legacy mindset of creating fans instead of customers no longer rewards a brand the way it once did. Some brands gradually identify this opportunity and take their thinking to a higher level. They satisfy the cultural need and recognize the market opportunity for meaningful, profound, personal connections. They build belonging.

In today's fast-moving and ever-changing environment, it is those companies that promote opportunities to create, sustain, and grow substantial relationships that will ultimately emerge as winners. A handful of premium brands are already one step ahead on this journey. Apple has rebranded its stores, calling them "town halls." Verizon has moved from thinking of itself as a premium communications brand to a company that builds the future. If belonging can be built around technology companies, it can most certainly be made in people-based businesses.

The bottom line? Society's most significant challenge today is that we are living in an age of deficit—a belonging deficit. It's no secret that we all crave to belong to something or someone: a movement, a group of people, or a system of beliefs. It's in our nature after all, and it hasn't changed much since the dawn of time. What has changed, at warp-speed pace, is how we connect with others.

If you're thinking, "Yeah, but I don't think that's necessarily a good thing," then you'd be right. We have shorter attention spans. Our lives are spent in front of screens. We are continually scanning, swiping, and clicking. Our attention divides so fast, and so frequently that we don't feel connected to any given experience. A recent study has shown an alarming increase in feelings of anxiety, loneliness, and disengagement, particularly among younger generations.

Even though technology plays a significant role in contributing to growing isolation, it is not the sole cause of it. A host of other factors affect the belonging deficit we are facing—decreased levels of trust with large institutions that once fostered community, growing economic inequality, and rapid political polarization among them. The problem is there, right in front of us, blatantly apparent for all to see—a belonging deficit exists, opening the door for someone to step in.

IN A STUDY OF 172 BRANDS:

TOP BRAND BELONGING PERFORMERS GREW REVENUE AT

3X

THE RATE OF BOTTOM PERFORMERS - OVER A 6 YEAR PERIOD

TOP PERFORMING BRANDS GAINED UP TO **10%** MARKET SHARE OVER A 3 YEAR PERIOD

INCREASING BRAND BELONGING CAN GROW REVENUE **12%** PER YEAR

BE/
LONG
/ING
FACTOR

"For all our differences, collectively, humans share a deep desire for connection, community, and a sense of belonging."

CHAPTER 3

The Past Informs the Present

(My Privilege)

"It is the highest form of self-respect to admit our errors and mistakes and make amends for them. To make a mistake is only an error in judgment, but to adhere to it when it is discovered shows infirmity of character."

— Dale Turner

WHETHER YOU received your degree in business from a prestigious university or the school of hard knocks, you acquired—at an elementary level—roughly the same set of information. I get that this statement is controversial, but bear with me. You learned the fundamental principles of measuring success, calculating and mitigating risk, managing processes, and leading people. You learned to create a strategy and what to do when things go wrong. You even learned the difference between a great leader and a poor one. While all the details you absorbed were inevitably diverse in nature, they share one similarity: In processing them, you learned to believe what you were taught.

This pattern is essentially the same for every person on the planet. We are taught from a very early age what is right and what is wrong, what to think, what to value, and what to believe. Likely the very first thing you were taught to know and to believe was your name. Think about it. You had no idea what you were called, or even that you were called something until you were told that you needed to respond when someone called you by your name. You believed, without question, that your name was yours. Your identity began to form around your belief in yourself, your name included. Isn't it baffling, the idea that your name—an integral part of your identity—was just something someone made up? They thought it sounded good and gave it to you, without knowing a single thing about your personality. Nevertheless, you believed it, and as you got older, you began to teach your name to others; first in school and sports, then in social settings and at work. You were taught what to believe, and you taught others to think the same.

This trivial example may seem a bit far-fetched to you. However, it illustrates rather clearly what you should remain consciously aware of as you continue forging your path in the world, influencing and inspiring others. You tend to believe what you are taught to understand and show it to others. It's a necessary skill to survive in a world governed by a multitude of rules and norms. Often, the first thing you read or hear about a topic sets an anchor, and you begin to solidify a system of beliefs around it. You observe the world and the people around you and start to model your ideas, thoughts, and behaviors of those whom you deem credible. It is how you define your beliefs. Although this is, in principle, a great trait and one that may have served you well throughout your life and in your career, it is crucial to be aware of the fact that there are likely some things you assume and teach others (because you believe them) that are the result of a bias that you may not even know you have.

As humans, we are afflicted with a predisposition to biases. Among the most common biases we encounter in our lives is confirmation bias. Once we have formed a view, we tend to embrace information that confirms that view while ignoring, or rejecting, information that casts doubt on it. Confirmation bias suggests that we don't perceive circumstances objectively. We pick out those bits of data that make us feel good because they confirm our inclinations, mindless of the fact that these are often prejudices of which we are unaware. Moreover, we risk becoming prisoners of our assumptions. However, what does all this have to do with belonging? A lot, actually.

My privilege

I was raised enjoying privileges a significant part of the population has no access to. I didn't grow up in a wealthy family or attend prestigious schools. I was not the proverbial Fortunate Son of money and power. No, my privilege was of a different kind. I was born a cisgender, straight, Caucasian male in the United States. So it strikes me now as quite remarkable that I was neither raised with an awareness of just how profound that privilege is nor with ignorance to the plight of others. I had no concept of the access, trust, and opportunity my gender and ethnicity afforded me.

Raised in Northern California by liberal-minded parents, I was regularly exposed to a diverse mix of cultures and languages. I didn't see myself as any different than those around me. What I wasn't aware of, however, was that I was being treated differently than those around me. It often happened when I wasn't around—when they were at the grocery store, the bank, or a restaurant. Of course, I never saw this. Even in a progressive and ethnically diverse state like California, the impact of white privilege was palpable just under the surface, hidden from my naive, young eyes.

At the age of eighteen, I enlisted in the U.S. Navy and "shipped off" to boot camp. This was my most memorable adult introduction to the privilege I was raised with. While it wasn't unusual for me to see faces that looked different from mine—our company barracks housed 64 young men from all over the country—it became clear to me that this wasn't the case for everyone in Division 195. I was selected as the first recruit in command of the division. Succeeding me was another white male—who went on to serve bravely as a Navy SEAL. The drill instructors charged with the selection of both of us were (no surprise here) both white men.

At the time, I barely noticed the preferential treatment I had received. I attributed it to my hard work and prior experience as a Sea Cadet. What I didn't know back then was that another recruit, José Garcia, had more experience than me as a Sea Cadet and outranked me by two grades. He was also in much better physical shape than I was at that time. This information was, of course, available to the drill instructors. Surprisingly, they did not give José the position.

Fast forward to where I sit today. After completing my service in the Navy, I spent the following twenty years in corporate America, becoming subtly aware, at first, of the privilege bestowed upon me. Over time, it slowly dawned on me that I had been living my life believing that everything I had earned, I earned the hard way—through grit, determination, preparation, and execution. I had carved my path—without help from any outside factors. My past had informed my present. I was the product of what was taught to me by my parents. People are people—how they look or what gender they may identify as is not an indicator of character or capability. I was raised to think I was the same as everyone else, and everyone was the same as me.

While the approach my parents took to raise me was incredibly well-intentioned and helped me treat others as equals and fellow humans, it lacked the foresight to prepare me for a complex and sometimes confusing world in which privilege affords the opportunity. Honestly, I'm not even sure how you would introduce such an intricate concept to a child. Maybe that's why we're all trying to figure this out like adults. What I do know is that once I became aware of my privilege, my world changed. The part of my past that was informing my present shifted. What shapes and affects me now are more recent experiences and lessons. The energy they release and the opportunities they provide are what enable me to help and influence others.

The fact that you're reading this book indicates a desire to do the same—and that's fantastic! We'd better get started because life doesn't pause to allow us time to catch up. The future is never as far away as we think. It will be here before we know it.

"The workplace of the future…is an inherently healthy environment that reinforces trust, compassion, respect, and understanding."

CHAPTER 4

Why the Future Can't Wait

"The power for creating a better future is contained in the present moment: You create a good future by creating a good present."

— *Eckhart Tolle*

WE'RE ALL on board with the facts here, right? A sense of belonging is a vital human need. When we don't feel as though we belong, we grow anxious and wary. We don't experience trust. We aren't the best version of ourselves. Also, we agree that the rate of loneliness in many workplaces is on the rise. In an age of diversity and inclusion, this isn't what we would expect to see, right? What cannot be denied is that policies on diversity and inclusion have their limits. They can provoke a desire to change, but that can only carry us so far. They must extend beyond weak attempts to pacify a social cause or fulfill a status requirement. What we must do—and this is crucial—is to help people understand and believe that they are valued and essential contributors within their teams. Pat Wadors, Chief Talent Officer at ServiceNow, quite rightly says:

> *"While diversity is what makes us each unique, our differences can be polarizing and create all sorts of challenges in workplaces despite the many benefits it brings. And while policies of inclusion can ensure everyone is invited to the dance, it's a sense of belonging that allows workers to feel safe, valued, and seen."*

A question people often ask me is, "Can't this wait? I have so many other priorities." At times, I'd love to answer, "Only if you hate yourself, your employees, and your organization." I don't. All sarcasm aside, I say, "No, it can't wait, because this is the future; it is here, and it is now!"

The workplace of the future (i.e., the present) is an inherently healthy environment that reinforces trust, compassion, respect, and understanding. It fosters the confidence that a person can be authentic and vulnerable at work. It creates energy, camaraderie, community, and engagement between colleagues. The future workplace elicits a feeling of psychological safety, which engenders a willingness to seek out and understand other opinions and perspectives. It spawns collaborators sharing aligned values that help their organization compete. It is a workplace that empowers people and drives profits.

Now stop and take a moment to reread that last paragraph. Underline or highlight something that is of paramount priority for you at this very moment; something that just isn't happening the way you think it ought to be. All right, all set? If your organization is like most, you've marked up nearly the entire paragraph. You likely have a trail of projects and programs in your wake—some successful and some not—that represent your best efforts to tackle these priorities. Well, that's a good thing. That means that you and your organization care enough to give it your everything. The time to get it right is now! That future we are supposed to be preparing for—that one where AI and technology outpace the capacity and capability of business—isn't waiting for you or anyone. It is right now.

A relatively small percentage of leaders have a clear understanding of this, and an even lower percentage of brands are prepared for this reality. Those who have championed the concept of and recognized the value in people-centric leadership and brand building have done much of the heavy lifting for the rest of us. They've pioneered previously uncharted territory, illuminating a path we can and should follow. Treading in the footprints left by early champions of diversity and inclusion is certainly a good start. Even so, we cannot merely expect that strategy alone to elevate our people and our organizations to their highest capabilities. It's time we all did our part to carve new paths by championing the most significant asset any organization has—its people.

Before unwrapping and defining the five characteristics of the Belonging Factor and strategizing on the next steps, I'd like you to consider how you, as an individual, would participate in or encourage others to contribute to building a sense of belonging in your organization. Create a shortlist, consisting of small actions that anyone in the organization, regardless of position or title, can put into place. I'll be so bold as to make a few recommendations to get you started.

1. **BE CURIOUS**
2. **PRACTICE GRATITUDE**
3. **ENGAGE IN DEVELOPMENT**
4. **SHARE YOUR STORY**

BE CURIOUS

Ask questions. Seek to understand others' views and perspectives. Eliminate criticism and focus on building constructive curiosity instead. Stop viewing mistakes as failures, but explore them through after-action reporting and dialogue, thus turning them into lessons that lead to future success. Give yourself and your people permission to evolve out of a comfort zone that prevents risk-taking and stifles innovation.

PRACTICE GRATITUDE

Reignite the flame of personal connection and humanity during your next team meeting. If you're a leader, ask your team to share personal or professional gratitude before starting the meeting. If you're a team member, ask for permission to express gratitude to a colleague and encourage others to do the same. This will allow for a mutual understanding of who you are, not just what you do for work.

ENGAGE IN DEVELOPMENT

Create a mentorship program or ask to be a peer coach. Take an active role in the development of others, help to unlock potential, and build on people's strengths and passions so that they can bring out the best in themselves. Make learning and sharing of information a priority.

SHARE YOUR STORY

We've all been there. We've encountered that moment when we felt as though we didn't belong; when we questioned our place in the world and wondered if we ever truly belonged. Moreover, we've equally all felt fulfillment and comfort when we experienced a sense of belonging. What's your experience? When you share your story of belonging, you share part of your personality, thus giving others the chance to see behind the curtain, to get to know you, to build connections, and to understand what belonging is all about. It's a gift that keeps on giving.

PART 2

THE BELONGING FACTOR

"The same elements that comprise the factor for leaders are the very same elements that comprise the factor for brand engagement and deep loyalty."

CHAPTER 5

The Belonging Factor Explained

"One of the things that are consistent amongst all great leaders is they're a great teammate that is invested in the guys around them to raise the level of play. You do that by believing in guys and caring about them."

— Sean McVay

THE BELONGING FACTOR is, at its foundation, a set of the five critical characteristics the most successful brands and leaders consistently demonstrate. They are a culmination of mindset and behaviors that create a sense of community, connection, belonging, inspiration, and value alignment. Organizations that possess these characteristics are some of the most profitable and successful organizations on the planet. Leaders who bring these characteristics to life are some of the most inspiring, rewarding, and accomplished leaders on Earth.

As you read and come to understand the elements that lay the foundation on which the Belonging Factor builds, keep in mind that, no matter if we're talking about a brand or a leader, no organization manifests these characteristics on its own. The Belonging Factor is a result of a deliberate effort by the people within the organization. The Belonging Factor is, in fact, about people.

When I began my quest to understand better what made the best rise to the top and stay there, and what made others fail to achieve their true potential, I examined hundreds of brands and leaders within a multitude of organizations. I studied leaders at all levels, from frontline to executive and C-suite leaders, who influence the lives and the work output of those in their charge. Patterns began to emerge that warranted further inspection. The deeper I looked, the more I found a shared set of principles, attributes, and behaviors that I describe as the Belonging Factor. The real magic here is this: The same elements that comprise the factor for leaders are the very same elements that comprise the factor for brand engagement and deep loyalty.

That said, the Belonging Factor is not a solution in itself. It is a deeply researched, profound understanding of qualities and ideas people share. Only when people like you decide to take action, can it become a resoundingly powerful solution. Simon Sinek is known to opine, "Great leaders are not born, they are developed." I find this to be an exceptionally exact sentiment, and the Belonging Factor serves as unequivocal evidence.

1. **DEFINE ROLES AND BEHAVIORS**

2. **BUILD INTELLECTUAL DIVERSITY**

3. **MODEL WHAT'S EXPECTED**

4. **EMPOWER OTHERS**

5. **FOSTER COLLABORATION**

These are the five characteristics the Belonging Factor is comprised of. There are sets of actions grouped around each of them. They are everyday occurrences reflected in the tone of an email, the way a brand responds to a customer, the format choice for advertising, how meetings are held, and how hiring decisions are made. Each moment of action is an opportunity to align with or not align with building a sense of belonging.

Later, we'll dive deeper into both a case for belonging in the workplace and a case for belonging in a brand. Before we get there, it is imperative to understand the underlying principles and actions associated with each characteristic. For each of the five observable characteristics, there are unobservable, but essential, principles that define, shape, and determine the behaviors that comprise individual elements of the Belonging Factor.

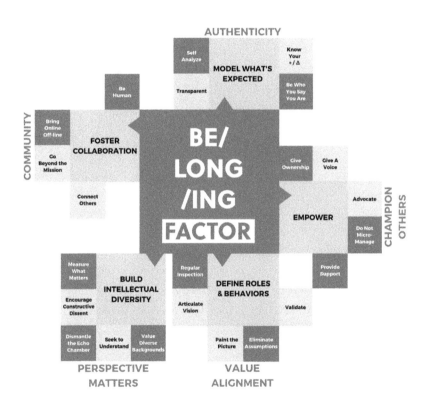

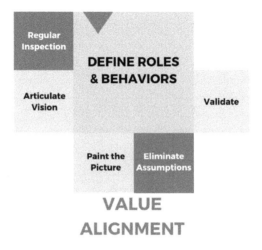

Let's look at the first characteristic: **DEFINE ROLES AND BEHAVIORS**. The underlying principle of this characteristic is **VALUE ALIGNMENT**.

As CEO of Populus Group, Bobby Herrera has faced his fair share of struggles. He chooses to look at each struggle as a gift and has been rewarded many times in his life for that approach. One example he shares is about the effort to build the culture he envisioned when he founded the company. Among the many lessons he learned along the way, he underscores the tremendous importance of over-communicating your vision and clearly defining how you expect your people to behave.

"Overcommunicate exactly how you expect everyone who is part of the culture to behave. Encourage your leaders to be unwavering in their demands about the company's principles."

Act on this advice, and you will all but eliminate any room for assumptions that would have otherwise inevitably filled the void left whenever communication lacks a clear definition of values and cultural expectations. When team members aren't clear on their organization's values, it can be exceedingly difficult for them to align their values and find the work they are doing to be rewarding.

Take the time to inspect the existing culture and validate that your values are understood throughout the organization and are being carried out in all interactions —be that among peers, communicating with clients, or in the boardroom—is mission-critical.

The second characteristic, **BUILD INTELLECTUAL DIVERSITY**, is based on the underlying principle of perspective, because **PERSPECTIVE MATTERS**.

Diversity and inclusion, exists as an overly broad term. It is defined differently by various organizations and people, and measured in a great many ways—some effective and some practically useless. Those leaders and brands who enjoy the highest loyalty do not measure the diversity of their team, their customers, their suppliers, or their leaders solely by their gender identification, race, socio-economic status, or any other superficial criteria. Instead, they understand intellectual diversity—diversity of thought and capability—is the one core element that elevates collaboration to a new level, thus building community, and enhancing performance.

It all begins with valuing diverse backgrounds and experiences. It requires your talent acquisition team and their respective process to be evolved enough to source and appropriately digest the information you need to make the right hiring decisions. Once on board the team, it requires a sincere desire to understand people— to go beyond the superficial. One of the most successful methods of doing this is to establish a culture that encourages constructive dissent. By hearing out different points of view which, by nature, are in disagreement with the consensus, employees are rewarded with the opportunity to give voice to their thoughts, while the organization learns to understand and accept that groupthink and silos do not have a place in corporate culture.

In my experience, there are countless occasions when employing this method is crucial to make sure mission-critical factors are kept up in order to avoid disaster. When the group signs off on a plan, but a brave dissenter offers constructive feedback, we are able to see possible flaws in an idea and make necessary adjustments. The converse cultural phenomenon is one of fear—when employees are afraid to express dissent for fear of reprimand or, worse, retaliation.

When appropriately executed, building intellectual diversity allows an organization to avoid one of the most destructive cultural forces—the echo chamber. Like a carbon monoxide leak, the echo chamber can go undetected until tragedy strikes. What is the echo chamber, and why should it scare the hell out of you?

AN ECHO CHAMBER IS A METAPHORICAL DESCRIPTION OF A SITUATION IN WHICH BELIEFS ARE AMPLIFIED OR REINFORCED BY COMMUNICATION AND REPETITION INSIDE A CLOSED SYSTEM. BY VISITING AN ECHO CHAMBER, PEOPLE ARE ABLE TO SEEK OUT INFORMATION WHICH REINFORCES THEIR EXISTING VIEWS, POTENTIALLY AS AN UNCONSCIOUS EXERCISE OF CONFIRMATION BIAS.

The dangers this effect harbors became evident to the public when Mark Zuckerberg, Chief Executive of Facebook, testified before Congress on the internal workings of his company that allowed for rampant abuse by foreign governments concerning elections in the United States. His testimony and the investigative journalism that followed gave the world astounding insights into an organization that had not only failed to embrace the values it proclaimed, but, more importantly, had not sought outside guidance on the issues they were experiencing. Making matters worse, the senior executives of the organization had been in their positions for five to seven years. This is not a common practice within the C-suite at companies on the magnitude of Facebook. Often, executives are cast in new leadership roles every year or two. It was widely reported, however, that Zuckerberg preferred to challenge the status quo—much to his chagrin. It was also widely reported that these executives insulated him from certain troubles within the organization to maintain their good standing and to not upset their CEO. In fairness to Zuckerberg, it needs to be said that he has now recast his executive staff and embarked on a culture revamp at Facebook since these issues were scandalously revealed to the public.

The moral of the story? Beware of and be prepared for the echo chamber effect. If you're only hearing good news, and everyone is always in agreement, you've got a problem. The inability to openly share grievances, relay problems, or provide critical feedback is a leading indicator of a lack of trust. It is also a clear sign that the echo chamber may be in full effect. Address it before it gets a chance to suck all the oxygen out of your organization, your people, and you.

―――――――

AUTHENTICITY

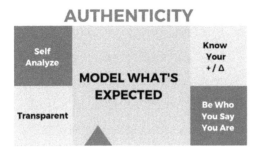

The third characteristic of the Belonging Factor, **MODEL WHAT'S EXPECTED**, is arguably the most critical. Great leaders do not ask of their people what they, themselves, are not willing to do. This is a time-tested factor of success. When applied to the Belonging Factor, the significance of this aspect is magnified, as it serves to tie each of the other four characteristics together, and reflects one of the most visible leadership qualities by which others judge, evaluate, and, ideally, emulate. It stands to reason that the underlying principle, **AUTHENTICITY**, holds significant value as well.

Authenticity is another one of those curious words left open to broad interpretation. More often than not, it is thrown about carelessly or misused to achieve the exact opposite of what it actually means. At the core, authenticity means to be who you say you are—to be the most authentic version of yourself. It means not trying to be what you think others expect of you or not changing something about yourself to fit each particular situation. In a brand, being authentic means knowing your actual values, recognizing whom you serve, and delivering every decision, every conversation, and every interaction in alignment with that. In a leader, it means understanding what your greatest strengths are, how easily they can turn in to weaknesses when overused or exposed to pressure and stress, and what to do about that.

Modeling what's expected equally requires a potentially uncomfortable level of transparency. You may be able to fool yourself, but you don't fool your people. They know when you are transparent and when you're not. While it's not always possible, or advisable to share every single detail with your team at every given moment, leaders who have built trust by being transparent, find themselves in a position to offer advice that might sound like this:

> *"We do have a series of changes that we'll be*
> *making to our organization over the next*
> *several months. While this is something*
> *we've anticipated as a result of our rapid*
> *growth, it is still change, and will likely come*
> *with moments of uncertainty. What I can*

assure you now, is that the conversations
we're having around what our future looks
like are encouraging. Once I'm able to share,
I will—but just know that the work you're
doing right now matters and will continue to
matter."

Taking the time to understand who you are as a leader, what your team needs from you, and how to best provide it is at the center of that great internal conflict all leaders face.

Within a brand, transparency is of paramount importance for potential and existing customers alike. In the age of the Internet of Things and ubiquitous digital connectivity, it has become fairly easy for a consumer to learn about supplier/vendor relationships, manufacturing processes, intra-corporate conflict, and questionable policies. Once discovered, that same connectivity allows any information to spread like wildfire and possesses the power to dismantle/destroy a brand in a matter of hours.

To maintain an awareness of how authentic and transparent we are is an incredibly difficult task to accomplish. The best brands and leaders manage it through impeccable self-analysis. Many organizations do this internally by analyzing and evaluating both customer and employee surveys and feedback. Experienced leaders do this on their own, through reflection and by asking themselves what impact their decisions had on their people and their people's performance—you might call it an *after-action report.* Consciously running through this process enables them to spot the characteristics and principles they demonstrate.

Much to my regret, we still operate in a world where few organizations and even fewer leaders bring this to bear. They tacitly accept their fate—they are destined to repeat the errors of their predecessors, and while the ensuing fatal consequences may not be immediately evident, their past will continue to inform their present.

If you're reading this book, I would readily accept the assumption that you have a vested interest in building that sense of true belonging—the Belonging Factor—in acquiring and mastering all these capabilities for yourself or for your organization. I would be glad to assume you understand that building a sense of belonging is vital to delivering long-term success because belonging builds connection; connection builds community; community inspires loyalty; loyalty implies value; and values drive productivity and profits.

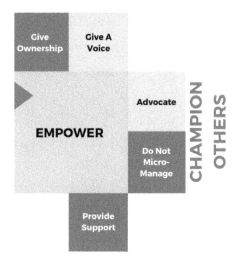

The characteristic that often provides the greatest emotional connection and deepest sense of belonging comes in at number four on the list. To **EMPOWER** inspires all parties involved, because of the associated principle, **CHAMPION OTHERS**, and the openly visible nature of the accompanying actions.

Some of the most iconic brands champion the cause of others in their advertising. While this may be a calculated decision deliberately made by their marketing department, it is often something that is derived from within and is driven by the people of an organization. Businesses that listen closely to these voices and operate in alignment with them have absolutely nailed it.

T-Mobile US, based in Seattle, Washington, solicited input from their employees regarding LGBTQ+ rights awareness during Pride month. They collected tons of suggestions and granted their employees the power to decide the ultimate path the organization would choose. Ideas ranged from rainbow flag-branded advertising and employee uniforms to allowing employees to participate in Pride parades in their community and lighting up the T-Mobile headquarters in Pride colors. Adding to the credit of T-Mobile's senior leadership team, they put all of the suggestions in practice—an extraordinary way to demonstrate a commitment to fulfilling a sense of belonging, isn't it?

Nike, on the other hand, took an incredibly controversial approach. The story of one of Nike's most controversial advertising decisions earned international media coverage in 2018. They chose to run an ad featuring Colin Kaepernick, former quarterback of the San Francisco Forty-Niners, who caused an uproar by deciding to kneel during the National Anthem before each game. He explained, quite articulately, that kneeling was his way of calling attention to the injustices that exist in criminal prosecution and policing in the United States. He offered this gesture as a silent protest to encourage dialogue around these issues.

While a great many people who witnessed his actions rallied behind him, a significant part saw it as an unforgivable act of disrespect—to the country that had afforded him the opportunity to become a professional athlete and earn millions of dollars. Detractors began posting videos on social media of them burning Kaepernick jerseys and piles of other Nike apparel. As is so often the case, they took to social media to express their outrage over Nike's championing of Kaepernick.

Regardless of where you may sit in that discussion, what is important to note here is that Nike took a stance to publicly champion—to support, advocate, and give a voice to—an athlete who decided to stand up for something that apparently aligned with Nike's brand values. So, why would they take such a risk?

Nike's stock prices took an immediate hit. However, they rebounded in a matter of days, without Nike backing off their beliefs or principles. They chose empowerment because it was in line with how they saw themselves as an organization. By deciding to champion Colin Kaepernick's message, as a brand, they didn't just empower one man, they triggered a flood of dialogue between millions of people. Nike created a buzz of water-cooler conversation across the globe about the issues Colin Kaepernick was willing to sacrifice his career for.

Let's explore this from a leadership perspective. To give ownership of a decision to your employees, rather than deciding for them, empowers them to own not just the decision, but the desired outcome. Giving a voice to individuals and the collective team encourages everybody to share their ideas, opinions, and processes. Maybe more meaningful is the importance of advocating for an employee who is facing a challenge, up for a promotion, struggling to meet a deadline, or is needing additional support education. Advocating for that employee lets them know that you're in their corner and you have their back, that you believe in them—an accurate representation of championing others.

Of course, not micromanaging the process does belong on this list. Nothing is less empowering than telling somebody what to do, how to do it, and then micromanaging every moment of how they're executing it. Despite plenty of research to clearly articulate the mess that is micromanagement, we still live in a world of many micromanagers. While this book does not attempt to solve the challenges and specific needs of those who have a tendency to micromanage, it can offer this: If you find yourself in that category, even if only at times of stress and pressure, understand that the decision to micromanage, removes empowerment, removes the championing of others, and therefore gets in the way of your ability to build that sense of belonging, community connection, and value. It is ultimately one of the most significant obstacles in your ability to deliver the profits that you would otherwise be capable of.

FOSTERING COLLABORATION is the fifth and last element that I attribute to leaders and brands demonstrating the Belonging Factor. This is where everything pays off. By commanding the concept of **COMMUNITY**, the underlying principle here, each of the other four characteristics becomes tangible through people's actions within the groups the Belonging Factor caters to. For a brand, that group is likely its customers. For a leader, it is most frequently their team and their cross-functional counterparts.

There are three core actions that enable you to cultivate cooperation and teamwork. You'll find that *being human* takes the top spot on that list. No matter your product or service; no matter your role or responsibility; regardless of your field of activity, whether you're in IT, sales, operations, hold an executive or administrative position—be human. It is impossible to feel connected to or feel a sense of community with someone who does not show their humanity. When you make a mistake, own it. If you're fallible, be fallible. Publicly own and accept that fact, address it, and move on. Smile, engage, ask questions, seek to understand and listen to your people, your customers, your boss—as an individual. At the end of every workday, every single person in your building, or all the buildings across your enterprise, goes home. They go back to friends, to family, to people—after all, they are a person too. It is far too dangerous to treat even one person as dispensable, or as just a part of the machine.

Go beyond the mission. What does that mean in a brand? It means doing social good and going beyond your task of selling your product or service to generate profit, while also being a good steward of your community. Anticipate your employees' wants and be there when they need you, without being asked. Offer some benefit that is usually not on the agenda or not even commonly offered in your industry. Make a conscious decision to look beyond the bottom line and instead at the people who are a part of your world.

As mentioned before, the near-complete digitalization of our lives poses quite a few challenges. That is why—bringing online connections offline—is more important now than ever. Successful brands understand this concept well. Bringing connections offline means bringing community offline. It's not just a matter of placing your product in a brick and mortar store. It's about bringing people together—connecting others—offline.

The fastest growing musical instrument manufacturer in the United States has managed to bring this to perfection. This is what Mike Ciprari, co-founder of SJC Drums, told me when I discussed this topic with him:

> *"We engage the vast majority of our customers online through social media, through our website, and through email. We reply to every one of them, but that's not enough. If we do something wrong, we make a point to make it right in the real world—not through a discount or waiving a fee."*

Ciprari shared an example of a particular customer, whose product delivery was going to be late. For him, that wasn't acceptable seeing that such delays are not the standard customers of SJC Drums are used to. What he did perfectly exemplifies the fifth characteristic of the Belonging Factor. Ciprari visited the customer's social media account and noticed that he was a huge Batman fan. Without hesitation, Ciprari decided to get a couple of very cool Batman trinkets, added a handwritten note of apology, and put them into the box when the merchandise was shipped. The cost/benefit ratio weighed entirely in SJC's favor. Not only did this small and easily accomplished gesture actively prevent a customer from being unhappy, it most probably also turned the Batman fan into a lifelong loyal customer.

If the connection to a customer is only existent online, the relationship between customers and brand will only ever scratch the surface—it will merely be transactional. If a competitor shows up with a better offer? Off they go. Therefore, it is imperative to plunge in a little deeper—and reach a little closer to what lies below the surface. Many brands are doing this by hosting customer-centric events—events that bring customers together as individuals and build a stronger, more profound sense of connection and community. Don't get me wrong, I don't mean just throwing a big party and inviting lots of people. What these brands do is find creative ways for people to meet and get to know each other offline. As opposed to online platforms, they create offline platforms, where the people themselves are the root and the reason of all activities transpiring while connecting.

As a leader, bringing online connection offline is primarily about understanding the place that digital connection and communication occupy, and knowing when to go there and when to have real conversations. Email has replaced much of the talking that used to happen on the phone, transforming the way we in which we make contact with others. However, over time, this has become burdensome and started feeling rather disconnected. We have seen large efforts just recently to replace email communication with applications in an attempt to reduce the number of emails an employee has to go sort and respond to. By giving their employees access to mobile apps like Slack and GroupMe, companies have once again changed the way people in their organizations interact.

The trap here is, by focusing on productivity and efficiency, technology has become a surrogate to meaningful dialogue and interaction. Leaders need to be aware of the impact this has. If email is the primary medium with which you interact with the people on your team—no matter how positive your words of praise and encouragement are, how much ownership you give them, or how fiercely you advocate for them—your efforts will fall flat. Why? Because human connection requires elements that are only superficially available online. The interaction must come offline, where moments of real conversation, genuine connection, and a community of people can be allowed to collaborate and coexist.

For those not managing remote teams, the limitations are of an entirely different nature. We tend to use digital communication with people in the same building, on the same floor, sometimes even in the same room, which proves that limitations are quite frequently of our own making. This phenomenon is clearly magnified generationally, with some preferring a high-touch and others a low-touch approach. There are four generations making up our workforce right now—some grew up with their smartphones ready any time and any place and some have never even heard of, let alone used, some of the digital tools and methods we have at our disposal to communicate with each other today.

No matter where technology will take us in the future, the basic human need to feel connected, to be empowered, to know our values align, and to be positive the people around us are authentic—is a need that will never subside. Therefore, it is just a matter of understanding how you tap into that need to foster collaboration and build community in the environment you're in, together with the people you look after and with those who look after you.

BE/
LONG
/ING

FACTOR

"What I'm interested in is people, their place in work, and how they shape it."

Chapter 6

A Case for Belonging in the Workplace

"In the workplace, we're taught to worry about what happens if we don't have full, complete knowledge of every detail. But if you create a culture and an environment that rewards people for taking risks, even if they don't succeed, you can start changing behavior."

— *Reshma Saujani*

ONE OF the greatest changes to the workforce in a generation has not been the results of advancement in technology or a resurgence of industrial reinvention. While both automation and AI are starting to show their long-term impact on the jobs available to us mortals, they aren't the change I am most interested in. What I'm interested in is people, their place in work, and how they shape it.

My generation and those that came before me received guidance to go to school, work hard, land a good job, and stay there until retirement. We were told to do our best to advance our career and make a decent living, including weathering the storms of horrible bosses, corporate politics, and misaligned values. Be loyal, and you will be rewarded with pensions or retirement benefits.

In one generation, those sacred traditions have been dealt a significant blow. The millennial generation showed that a different reality is possible. We now operate in a reality in which collecting knowledge and experience from several companies, leaders, and job responsibilities are more valuable—to the individual and, arguably to the organizations as well.

What conditions must exist to attract and retain the best talent in this environment? The short answer: It's simple, but it is not easy. You can download your free copy of the checklist I use, simply by visiting book.belongingfactor.com. It's an easy-to-use format, with a simple set of behaviors and conditions required to create the environment you want. I can attest—from my personal experience, and that of my clients—it requires commitment, effort, and diligence to see through. Be careful not to force it. Don't rush the outcome. My best advice is to take it slow because slow is smooth and smooth is fast.

LANE STEEL CO., INC.

Lane Steel Company, Inc. was founded in 1982 in western Pennsylvania. A family-owned company, it was born into creation by Al Gedeon, a veteran of the steel industry in Pittsburgh. The "Steel City," as it is known, had seen the boon of steel fade away by that time. The steel mills and foundries were nearly all closed, with global competition applying unbelievable pressure. However, Al wasn't dissuaded. He believed in people and wanted to employ as many as he could, to deliver the product he knew like the back of his hand.

Fast forward to 2019. Paul Gedeon, Al's son, now helms the company. As I sat with Paul, discussing the culture of his company and why he thinks they've been able to survive in an industry that has been decimated by global competition, one thing became evident. The people of Lane Steel Company are committed to the vision, the leadership, the product, the customer—and each other.

Before expanding on the impact a sense of belonging has had on the company, I'd like you to get an understanding of the work environment the majority of employees experience daily. The picture below represents one section of the shop floor at Lane Steel Company. The shop is loud, hot in the summer, and cold in the winter. It is filled with heavy equipment, potential safety hazards, and spans hundreds of thousands of square feet. It is far from the realm of quaint offices with meditation rooms and coffee bars. There is no game room or massage hour. There isn't a Michelin star chef on staff to prepare meals. It is a harsh environment, where hard work and determination are the requisites.

What the picture doesn't show is the sense of purpose, pride, and belonging that each person feels. It doesn't demonstrate the commitment to the people that have propelled Lane Steel Company to success, nearly 40 years after it first opened its doors. To understand those dynamics, I had to speak with Paul Gedeon, president of the company.

Like many commoditized industries, global pricing instability places dynamic pressure that creates high highs and very low lows. Gedeon and many of his employees have ridden the waves of jubilation and despair because one thing remains true—everyone matters to one another. As a family-owned business, every employee knows the others. Executive, sales, administrative, and manufacturing teams work closely together. It's not just a family-owned business; it is a "family operated" business. It operates as a family.

The most remarkable lesson Gedeon offered me isn't complicated or even difficult. It's merely a matter of being human—intentionally—and regularly. He shared the story of reflecting on what he could do to inspire his employees during the tougher times, and how he might be able to retain the best people nonetheless.

Paul Gedeon always considered himself a man of the people. From his early start at the company to his role at the helm, he took care to remain visible and present on the shop floor and in the office. Gedeon made a point to "walk the shop" several times each week, offering a greeting as he passed by his people. Upon his reflection, he came to understand this, while well-intentioned, was merely transactional. Sure, it was good practice—one that many company presidents often overlook—but it lacked depth, connection, and appreciation for the richness of the person on the other end of the handshake.

Rather than devise an elaborate process in which to "get to know" each other better, Gedeon decided to evolve from "walk the shop" to "talk the shop." His plan was simple. No longer interested in transactional leadership, he aimed to connect, understand, involve, and champion his people. In the following weeks, he stopped and talked for a few minutes with each person he encountered. Dispatching with the usual pleasantries, he asked questions to understand better who his people were, what mattered to them, and what they needed from him.

What grew from this small change was a sense of trust and connection that helped carry the company through some of its most bleak quarters. Gedeon understood the unique, untapped talents of many of his people, and provided a platform for them to develop them. The employees brought a renewed energy and commitment to their work and each other. When a problem surfaced, the tendency to blame or hide disappeared. What replaced it was ownership, personal accountability, and collaborative problem-solving.

As I mentioned, while this was undoubtedly simple, it wasn't necessarily easy. It meant each conversation that inspired action also required follow-up. It also said that even when the feedback was tough to hear, it needed to be addressed appropriately—talking the shop required intention and dedication.

What does your version of "talk the shop" look like? How can you make a small but deliberate change to your engagement process to better foster a sense of community, connection, and belonging?

"While culture can start as one person's vision, it only thrives when those who live, work, or play in the culture can shape and grow it."

CHAPTER 7

A Case for Belonging in a Brand

"Companies and their brands need to reach out and speak directly to consumers, to honor their values, and to form meaningful relationships with them. They must become architects of community, consistently demonstrating the values that their customer community expects in exchange for their loyalty and purchases."

— Simon Mainwaring

AN AMERICAN brand has been hard at work, building belonging, to emerge as an overnight success nearly 20 years in the making. From refinishing drums in grandma's basement to a multimillion-dollar international custom drum company, SJC Drums built their success by putting the customer at the center of every decision. The following tale illustrates the power this brand wields.

On a brisk Saturday afternoon in the Northeast, Jason was walking down the street, clutching his cup of coffee to stay warm, on his way to work. Approaching him on the sidewalk, he saw something he recognized, a logo on a hat. He checked the face just beneath the brim but didn't know the man with the long salt-and-pepper beard wearing it. Although this man was a stranger, he didn't hesitate when the distance between them closed to a few feet to say, "Hey, man, nice hat!" The man with the beard stopped and said, "Thanks. Are you family too?" "Oh yeah!" was Jason's reply. This brief exchange between Jason and the man with the long salt-and-pepper-beard led to a ten-minute conversation about a company offering a fantastic product, inspiring leadership and a great work environment. It also led to the two exchanging numbers and forming what has by now become a four-year friendship.

So, what kind of hat was that? How is it that a logo on a hat can have the power to connect people in an instant? In such a profound way? The answer to that question is a matter of understanding both what and who is behind the company represented by that logo.

Of course, the logo on the hat was that of SJC Drums. On the surface, they appear to be like any other custom drum builders who craft high-end precision instruments made to match their customer's exact specifications. When taking a closer look, it doesn't take long to realize that there is much more to SJC Drums than that. After all, Jason and the man with the beard wouldn't have been able to form a direct and lasting bond based solely on their liking the same instrument manufacturer, would they?

What is it that SJC Drums has been able to do that other brands have not? What is their secret sauce? Ultimately it comes down to building a sense of belonging. That sense of belonging exists at the core of the company internally. From ownership to A&R to design and fabrication, every employee feels like they belong. Working at SJC Drums isn't like being a part of something; it's like being a part of a family. This sense of belonging extends externally as well. Customers of SJC Drums feel the same. That feeling builds a deep loyalty and sense of community not often seen outside of companies like Harley-Davidson, Apple, and Amazon.

It's no surprise to learn the corporate values of SJC Drums (Culture, Quality, Identity) align both internally and externally. In examining where the sense of belonging is developed in this environment, one need not look further than the simplicity and clarity of these values.

CULTURE

Culture has been the buzzword in boardrooms and management seminars for years—to little avail in many of the most established corporate bureaucracies. Action plans are created, and management training is implemented, under the misguided belief that a culture can be mandated. While culture can start as one person's vision, it only thrives when those who live, work, or play in the culture can shape and grow it.

Mike Ciprari, co-founder of SJC Drums, puts it this way:

> *"Culture is huge—inside and out. Fostering a culture where people feel welcome and part of the bigger picture empowers employees and attracts new customers. The family vibe spreads through and makes people feel personally accountable, increasing efficiencies*

> *and pride. It impacts the marketing and*
> *product design process by putting ourselves*
> *in the customers' shoes."*

In short, culture is a reflection of values in action. It is built to satisfy a need for belonging by those who want to belong. SJC gets this one right. SJC Drums is a close-knit family. When you purchase their drums, you truly become part of the brand. Every customer is just as important as the next, no matter who they are. SJC Drums represents some of the biggest names in the music industry like Tré Cool of Green Day; Josh Dun of Twenty One Pilots; Jay Weinberg of Slipknot; Daniel Platzman of Imagine Dragons; Dan Pawlovich of Panic! at the Disco, Frank Zummo of Sum 41, and many more. What makes the brand truly special is that these artists are promoted and supported in the same fashion as any other customer, no matter their background or level of playing. That means that a beginner in their first band is getting the same promotional support, social media shout outs, and product support as musicians at the top of their craft. Not only is this unheard of in the music industry, but it is also unheard of in most industries.

It doesn't stop there at SJC Drums. During an interview on the *Belonging Factor* podcast, Ciprari discussed the importance of building community and connection as part of the culture.

> *"We respond to every point of contact. If you hit us up on social media, email, it doesn't matter, we respond. If you tag us in a post, we make sure to like the post and comment and interact. We promote your band's shows or new album. We shout our artists out on their birthday. We encourage everyone in the family to support each other, and they do. It's super rad to see the community that exists out there. This really is a family. We think about it that way, and that's what makes this so rewarding for me and for all of us at SJC."*

Identity

If you want to challenge yourself or anyone in your professional or personal life, for that matter, ask this question: Can you describe your identity—who you are to yourself and those in your life? It's more challenging than you might think, to succinctly bring your identity into perspective. While it may be a challenge, it's absolutely something that must be done by any leader, in any organization intent on building a sense of belonging. Here's what SJC Drums has to say about their identity:

> *Whether you are buying your first drum kit or you're a seasoned drummer touring the world, we are here to help bring your dream drums to life. We build drums that stand out and turn heads. We want our drums to be an extension of the player's personality and to embody the innovative values that SJC Drums strives for in every build.*

Why would a for-profit brand put so much work into building belonging? The simple answer is because of the deep brand loyalty it engenders and the commercial opportunities it creates. In this crisis of belonging, great brands will step into the vacuum created by social isolation, and they will be significantly rewarded.

To learn more about building a brand that inspires profound loyalty, visit book.belongingfactor.com.

"People will always show you who they truly are. No matter the words that are spoken, paying attention to the behaviors and actions they exhibit will provide you authentic truth."

Chapter 8

Authenticity and Other Sh!t to Consider

"Authenticity doesn't just mean you're not filtering what you're saying, it's about being able to know and access the best parts of yourself and bring them forward."

— *Amy Cuddy*

HAVE YOU ever been in dialogue with someone you barely knew, when suddenly your bullshit detector lit up like a Christmas tree? How about when you were talking with someone you've known for quite some time? Was the bullshit meter slower or faster to move with the stranger or the longtime acquaintance? The

1. **WHEN SOMEONE SHOWS YOU WHO THEY ARE, BELIEVE THEM!**

2. **TRUST BUT VERIFY!**

bullshit detector is just a colloquial slang for our internal authenticity test. So, how do we test for authenticity?

If I told you that mixing red and blue paint would create a brilliant shade of orange, you'd raise the bullshit flag on me right away. Everyone knows that red and blue make purple. We were taught this in grade school, and haven't ever forgotten it. You can easily verify that my assertion is just flat out wrong. However, what happens if I say it over and over again? What happens if I start hanging pictures all over the place that show red and blue mixing to create an orange hue? What happens if this continues for years, with fewer and fewer people stopping to independently verify, instead of relying on what they see around them regularly?

This scenario plays out daily with both people and organizations who have the best of intentions, but flawed execution. It shows up in boardrooms and breakrooms across the world. The consequences of this type of environment being allowed to exist in business can be disastrous to culture, customer relationships, and shareholder return. Clearly, being able to identify whether a company or an individual is bullshit or the real deal is a critical skill—one that, when used properly, has the power to change your life.

Great news! There is a simple test you can use to answer the bullshit vs. real deal question. Two of the most exceptional pieces of advice I've ever received in my life form the basis for this test.

WHEN SOMEONE SHOWS YOU WHO THEY ARE, BELIEVE THEM!

People will always show you who they truly are. No matter the words that are spoken, paying attention to the behaviors and actions they exhibit will provide you authentic truth. This same concept also applies to organizations, both large and small. No matter how brilliant the vision, mission, or corporate values of an organization might be, the way a company treats its employees and its customers will always provide a more evident truth than words alone. Believe their actions. Always.

TRUST BUT VERIFY!

Be it words, or better yet, actions that you trust when forming your evaluation of a person or organization's bullshit level, be sure to take the next step. Verify. Verify, through evidence testing. This sounds rudimentary, and it is. However, the most basic of fundamentals are often the most sound, and simple to execute. What you see on the surface only represents a small part of the picture. Dig deeper. Ask critical questions. Seek essential evidence. Verify authenticity. Eliminate the bullshit.

Like the mixing of paint colors, to form a new color, somewhere in the combining of a person's (or organization's) words and actions is the evidence of their values. Imagine the blue color represents words (organizational values, mission, credo, etc.), and the red color represents actions and behaviors. Many things that are said will not align with behaviors, and several practices will not always sync with what is spoken or written. That space where the colors overlap—the rich purple—then represents the alignment of words and actions—an accurate representation of values. Values are evident at the intersection of words and actions.

In the ideal situation, the purple is rich and voluminous, almost entirely blending away the blue and red that formed it. A near-complete overlap of words and actions is representative of a bullshit-free test result. A minimal overlap, producing just a small, dull purple, leaving many words and many behaviors unaligned, paints a clear picture—the bullshit is thick.

I recently performed this test for an organization that was shedding its most talented, ethical, high-performing employees, while bleeding customers and losing market share in longstanding stronghold markets. When I listened to the leadership talk, they said all of the right things. They spread the corporate gospel (culture, diversity, customers, performance, integrity, etc.) with great fanfare. They expressed their belief over and over that they were the best, they were doing it the right way, and they were winning. The problem was that the words were hollow, bouncing off customers who had lost faith and employees who felt unheard, unvalued, and unimportant. Customers and employees (the good ones) felt like they belonged somewhere else, so they began to leave.

In running the bullshit test on the organization, several things became immediately evident.

• Trumpeting culture turned in to playing favorites. This showed up in performance evaluations, daily management, accountability actions, and promotions.

• The diversity initiatives, while well-intentioned, grew over the years to exclude large groups of employees rather than become an inclusive and collaborative experience. This wore on productivity, engagement, and left some of the brightest and most reliable feeling as though they couldn't carry the flag for the organization when things got tough.

• Customers, becoming frustrated at paying premium prices but receiving only average service, and being sold items they never wanted, began to explore other options. As they shared their new experiences with colleagues, family, and friends, more and more customers began to abandon the company.

• Policies, sales targets, and performance incentives were instituted that required the very best, most talented employees to be able to deliver in an ethical way. Unfortunately, the company had already lost the best, so it served its customers with the loyal. This created an environment where integrity all but disappeared, but performance improved—in a few categories in particular. The problem—very few in the leadership team asked why. They instead rewarded those who had top performance with awards and promotions, further promulgating a dangerous and defective culture that did not align with their stated values.

• Politics became the driving force at the director level and above. Understanding that many companies are not immune to this phenomenon, this company had seemingly completely abandoned the notion of brightest and best, in favor of fiercely loyal.

It is dismaying to witness this happening to companies with such powerful and unique visions, missions, and corporate culture statements. The color purple should have been omnipresent here, a magnificent deep shade of purple. Instead, red and blue didn't blend. This organization's actions and words were in no way aligned—despite the best efforts made by senior leaders to implement programs and systems to blend them flawlessly. What I found was that adding to the problem itself and making things worse was the senior management level—where it was common practice to withhold information and manipulate the truth if it served one's own purposes. Playing politics was rewarded. Honesty was viewed as being disloyal— particularly if it didn't align with a leaders personal views. As expected, this pattern spread downward to associate director and manager levels. It became commonplace to "put on the dog and pony show" when senior executives visited, so they would move on without incident. Well, I guess this is what everyone calls a toxic work environment these days.

BE/
LONG
/ING
FACTOR

PART 3

LIVING THE FACTOR

"If you truly want to understand your organization's culture, you must first start with its values."

CHAPTER 9

Operational Objectives

Organizational Values

---

*"Willingness to change is a strength,
even if it means plunging part of the
company into total confusion for a
while."*

— *Jack Welch*

AS YOU begin working on your plan to integrate the Belonging Factor into your processes, you'll likely feel the urge to operationalize certain aspects. Pause. Read through this chapter first. One of the single most significant mistakes made by companies as they integrate diversity, inclusion, and belonging into their organizational values is the reflex to codify or operationalize it. It's an instinct—everything a company wants to do a specific way ends up in Ops Manuals, SOPs, and M&Ps. Because that's the way things are done, and always have been. Again, pause.

Whenever a new process is established, we tend to start thinking about what objective measurements can be used to track progress. Will quarterly reviews reflect these metrics? If so, you'll have to set targets. So this, folks, is where the best of intentions becomes a self-inflicted wound—and turns out to be the opposite of what you intended. What you'll need to do is make a distinction between your organizational values and your operational objectives. I like to separate these two aspects this way:

ORGANIZATIONAL VALUES

If you truly want to understand your organization's culture, you must start with its values. Values determine the definition of good and bad. Values are at the heart of every culture. It is values that form and shape the way we work and live. They are an organization's lifeblood.

Values state what is important to you as an individual and what is important to your organization.

In other words, values are what you stand for. They reflect who you are, which in turn affects what you do and how you do it—this is your culture.

OPERATIONAL OBJECTIVES

Operational objectives are short-term goals which, once attained, bring an organization closer to its strategic, long-term goals. They identify a clear and measurable outcome of a business operation or process. Operational objectives outline specific tasks and incremental targets that need to be achieved in order to move the organization closer toward its long-term goals.

SEPARATING THE TWO

If your values guide your culture and your objectives are measures of success, these two concepts are invariably linked. So why not lump them together? Simple. Each aspect requires entirely different approaches to building the sense of belonging you desire, and the increase in productivity, contribution, and profits that come with it.

Here's a story to illustrate my point. While the names have been changed, the story is excruciatingly, and yet reassuringly real.

The story of Company X

Company X is a great company. Through mergers, acquisitions, and strategic partnerships, it has grown to over 100,000 employees. It delivers products and services worldwide but primarily operates in the United States. Although its legacy and operational mindset go back nearly 100 years, the brand we see and know today is merely decades old.

In the last two decades, Company X was known for innovation and reliability. It operated in the trenches, with an aggressive, performance-driven culture. That culture helped it grow as quickly as it did, but it also chewed up and spit out more people than it lifted to the top. It didn't actually lift *anyone,* let alone to the top. Chasing a promotion meant being politically cunning, self-serving, and delivering results at all costs. It wasn't just those with career ambitions who recognized that. It was well-known by and affected everyone within the organization. It impacted decisions to speak up (or not), and decisions to contribute or hold back. The corporate culture became toxic. In time, results began to plateau, then fall. One bad quarter led to another, and finally turned into a bad year.

To give the company's leaders credit, they recognized the need for change. What's more, they recognized the need for cultural change. Fortunately, they had always had a strong sense of how their organizational values drove their culture—sensing whether those values were being reflected in their employees' behaviors was an entirely different story. As was the fact that they were lacking something important. What they didn't provide for in their culture was—wait for it—diversity. So they rolled out their diversity initiatives.

Managers were given guidance on metrics. They were told how many people of color (POC) and how many gender diverse (the note actually read: women) employees they had on their teams. They were shown graphs and charts about how they stacked up against market and company averages. They were praised for being *above average* and coached if they were below average. While they were not assigned specific targets for POC or gender diversity—that would be entirely illegal—they were sent to training in order to uncover their biases, fueled by the misguided notion that different-looking people foster a more collaborative and productive culture. I shit you not.

Sure enough, Company X had managed to take an organizational value—a more diverse workforce, representative of the communities they serve—and turn it into operational objectives. Managers of locations where their population was over 90% single race, were admonished for having a 10% POC mix because the company average was 34%. Moreover, the talent acquisition teams began filtering out candidates who would do nothing to "diversify" the teams, passing only those candidates onto managers who would add to the POC or gender diverse mix, regardless of qualification. Of course, they wouldn't admit to that directly—again, that would be entirely illegal—but they couldn't hide the applicant data either. One can't make this stuff up. It's mind-boggling, isn't it? What makes this slightly less—or more terrifying— is that Company X truly is a fictitious organization. While the company is made-up, the story and data are not. Company X is an amalgamation of six different companies I studied for this book.

However, if you have been reading this and are dumbfounded about the fact I just perfectly described your company, that's probably because—and this is a terrible shame—there are thousands of organizations that operate in a similar way. Unfortunately, the fact that organizational values become KPIs on someone's performance review is often not a deliberate decision or intention. It is a result of conditioned behaviors and habits (the way things are always done), laziness (uninspired staff), and a blatant lack of identification with or understanding of the values a company's culture is meant to represent. It is quite simply a leadership issue. People working in a culture that places organizational values at the center of their decision-making process would never allow this to happen.

Getting it right

Don't get me wrong. I'm not saying evaluating the diversity of your team is not important. However, in order to do so properly, all relevant data must be considered. In particular, I champion the diversity of thought over almost all else. An organization whose employees all look different but think and act the same does not stand a chance against the competition. On the other hand, an organization like Populus Group does. What CEO, Bobby Herrera, and his "climbers" have all understood is that diversity of thought, background, experience, and ideology are the right ingredients for a healthy culture based on strong organizational values. Hence, operational objectives aim at impacting customers, developing products, and streamlining operations. People become the mechanism to deliver on these ideas.

The existing culture at Populus Group serves as a masterclass in building a sense of belonging and purpose, and creating a culture of shared values and mission alignment. Every one of the employees—they're called "climbers" at Populus Group—was selected because they demonstrated a distinct willingness to learn and teach during their interview process. Corporate culture at Populus Group expects climbers to share thoughts and ideas freely, from day one. Any ideas are welcome and will be heard and respected— what an excellent way to build trust. It is imperative that climbers are open to feedback and coaching and willing to step out of their comfort zone regularly. This holds for every member of the team, regardless of title or experience.

What employees at Populus Group experience, as a result, is the feeling to have a common purpose, faith in their fellow climbers and a sense of community and connection that allows them to be their best self every day. They are innovators who roll up their sleeves to get the job done. They are also humans—to each other, their clients, and of course, their families. What's interesting and rather unusual here is that Populus Group fully supports the maxim that the most important things in their employees's lives should come first (hint: Herrera doesn't expect it to be their careers). The company's guiding principle, the one that guides every detail of the organization is: give more than you take. This philosophy enables people to seek more and to contribute more in the world—for their clients, their fellow climbers, and in their community. The magic here is that operating this way and living this principle is that when everyone is operating in that manner, great things come back to each individual as well. Think of it as creating good karma.

You can find exercises that will help you clearly define (or redefine) your organizational values by visiting book.belongingfactor.com. You'll also find an activity that can help you untangle your operational objectives from your corporate values, should you find yourself in that situation (hint: once you look, you'll realize you're probably there—at least in a few areas).

"What we're trying to tap into is the value system we possessed at that age, before we became conditioned to the harshest realities of our world."

CHAPTER 10

What Would Your 12–Year–Old Self Think?

"Over time, naturally, you lose your innocence from gaining knowledge. You can't be innocent forever, but there's something in innocence you need to regain to be creative."

— *Albert Hammond, Jr.*

DURING THE course of an interview for the *Belonging Factor* podcast, SJC Drums co-founder Mike Ciprari discussed an approach he takes to maintaining perspective of what matters, in the face of running a multimillion-dollar business.

> *"I think back to when I was 12 years old. I*
> *wonder, what would 12-year-old Mike think?*
> *If he would think it's pretty rad, then hey,*
> *let's do this. But if 12-year-old Mike thinks*
> *this would suck, then you know what, maybe*
> *we shouldn't do it."*

There's something honest and refreshing about this perspective. Upon first examination, it seems unsophisticated and lacking in depth necessary to drive exceptional decision-making. The 12-year-old version of ourselves lacked the type of business savvy we inevitably possess at our current age. So, why listen to that *kid*? Honestly, there's a hell of a lot more our 12-year-old selves might be able to tell us about the most essential, *unspoken* element of the Belonging Factor— how we treat other people.

The perspective you're aiming for in an exercise like this isn't to evaluate the financial or legal liabilities associated with the ideas of your 12-year-old self. What you're trying to tap into is the value system we possessed at that age, before we became conditioned to the harshest realities of our world. What was important to us at that age? What motivated and excited us? What innocence did we possess to limit the filters we viewed the world through? I've done my best to capture that version of myself through an exercise I call, Return to 12. What follows is my interpretation of the answers I provided in that exercise. After you finish this chapter, I would encourage you to pause and reflect on this exercise yourself. You can find the Return to 12 worksheets and several other digital resources at book.belongingfactor.com.

My worldview as a 12-year-old was incredibly simple. I idolized a few celebrity musicians and wanted to emulate them. I didn't care about their race, religion, ethnicity, or education. I saw their talent, and I gravitated to it. I wanted to meet them and, of course, be like them. As a drummer myself, I was fascinated by Dave Abbruzzese, the drummer for Pearl Jam, at the time. I really, really, wanted to meet him. I wanted to be just like him. I thought that if I played the same drums like him, and I played the same style that he played, that I could somehow be connected to him. I told you it was a simple view.

In its purest form, my approach was this: If I thought it was cool, I wanted more of it. If I didn't think it was cool, I didn't want anything to do with it. I didn't spend a bunch of time talking negatively about it. I didn't go out there and try and figure out how to make it cool. I didn't want anything to do with it. Quite a narrow scope, but not atypical for a 12-year-old boy. From this understanding, I needed to understand what else was essential and why.

Upon reflection, I identified that it was important that other people thought I was cool. It brought a sense of pride, connection, and accomplishment. If someone didn't like me or something I was doing, I wanted to know why. I wanted to "fix it" and change so people would like me. So, while the superficial nature of my *why* was misguided, there was a sense of caring about *how* I impacted others. Interesting.

I was also a person who didn't apply limits to myself. At the age of 12, I believed I could do anything. I networked and eventually connected with Dave Abbruzzese. It was a truly magical moment. I kept playing drums, first emulating his style, then eventually developing my voice behind the kit. I've played with bands all over the world and had the time of my life doing it. More importantly, I found fulfillment in connecting with others, through music, building life-long relationships within the community.

How does this reflect in my current life? With the *Belonging Factor* podcast, I take pride in always improving the quality of production and content. I strategize and plan partnerships, advertisers, and format. However, those are all things my 12-year-old self wouldn't think is cool. He would think that adding value and connecting with my listeners is pretty cool, and that has informed how I prioritize my actions. When I receive a listener email, I reply right away. When someone messages me on social media, I follow up immediately. That's the kind of response I wanted from the people I was reaching out to when I was 12. I would have found it incredibly cool, if the people whose stuff (everyone just calls it "content" nowadays) I liked would have gotten back to me right away when I reached out to them.

Content. Everyone talks content. Relevant content. And rightly so. What would my 12-year-old self have to say about content curation for the *Belonging Factor* podcast? Remember, at 12, my worldview was simple, which is why I liked content that was relevant—to me that is. I would listen to the same few records over and over again. My parents would beg me to turn it off or put on headphones. I loved it, because each time I listened to these fantastic songs, I would find different parts in this one guitar sound or realize that there was this cool little fill that the drummer did. Whether it was the fourth or fortieth listen, I would always enjoy it for a new reason. Therefore, when curating content for the podcast, I go back and gut-check against my 12-year-old self to ensure I'm delivering content that is meaningful and relevant, and provides something new and insightful each time someone listens to it, no matter if it's the fourth or the fortieth time.

It's now time to ask yourself what you would think is super cool about your business. How would that inform your interactions with people and the decisions you make? What about the opposite—there must be a few things 12-year-old you would think are pretty lame. How would adopting this viewpoint provide the insight you aren't already considering? Remember, perspective matters!

Return to 12 is not an exercise specifically aimed at people running a business. It has the power to impact all of us and all aspects of our lives in many ways. We can use it to make a difference in the lives of those who we interact with, to unlock and to develop their potential to achieve more—be it as a little league coach, as a mentor, as a peer coach, a boss, a big brother, a husband, a wife, a sister, or as a friend There are so many ways that we can create and unlock this great potential to help people do more in the world.

BE/
LONG
/ING
FACTOR

"What should be inextricably clear at this point, is that the old way—emphasizing outcomes and results before all else—is not only bad for people, but it's just plain bad for business."

Chapter 11

A Practical Approach to People, Process & Profits

---

*"Empathy begins with understanding
life from another person's perspective.
Nobody has an objective experience of
reality. It's all through our own
individual prisms."*

— *Sterling K. Brown*

IN WRITING *Belonging Factor: How Great Brands and Great Leaders Inspire Loyalty, Build Community, and Grow Profits*, I deliberately only discussed profits early in the book; partially to grab your attention—the numbers are impressive—mostly to emphasize people and process. Each section and each chapter was designed to provide a different perspective or dive deeper into those two elements.

What should be inextricably clear at this point, is that the old way—emphasizing outcomes and results before all else—is not only bad for people, but it's just plain bad for business. Now, it should be said that I do tend to get a ton of shit for that last statement. For some reason, it is still controversial to encourage people to simply look after people first, and let the rest fall in place. Some people take it incredibly personally when I say that, acting as if I'd just told them to jump off a bridge. What's so offensive about suggesting everyone be decent to one another?

Now, you should also start to find the clarity that those organizations that have evolved to place people at the center of their values have developed a culture that has turned a sense of belonging into a profit driver. The examples shared by SJC Drums, Lane Steel Company, and Populus Group are evidence that any brand, organization, or leader that holds this principle dear will thrive. The storms that any organization weathers are often shorter and less tumultuous because everyone is committed to the same values and same outcome. There isn't a need to force compliance or bend the will of others to get the job done. While it's not always smooth sailing, it surely isn't volatile and unpredictable.

Now, the practical approach to people, process, and profits. On the following page, I've simplified the Belonging Factor map for easy application in virtually any situation. Think of this approach as a "gut check" exercise that can be used in any conversation or at any decision point.

- Instead of asking if something fosters collaboration and builds community, just ask, does this bring people together?

- Rather than wrapping yourself up in worrying about if you're modeling what's expected, just be a good person.

- One of the best ways to empower and champion others is simply to look for a reason to celebrate instead of criticizing.

- Don't let a single opportunity pass to align values and define roles and behaviors. A simple method is to build the reflex to make sure people know what's right.

- Building intellectual diversity is not only important but highly beneficial. One of the easiest ways to ensure you're on the right path is to *beware of the echo chamber*. If you seem to be hearing the same ideas and constant agreement, you know where to take action.

These practical steps are my best suggestions today. They're based on personal experiences and the experiences of other great leaders, who've learned to pour their energy into what matters most. It's important that whether you choose to use the suggestions offered here, or create your own, you make a habit of the elements that are the Belonging Factor. I encourage you to make it your own. Create an acronym or other mnemonic devices that work for you, because while the process is simple, it isn't easy.

Any time you're retraining your behavior, or introducing new behavior expectations to others, it takes diligence and intention over time. Don't rush it. Remember, slow is smooth and smooth is fast. Have patience with yourself and those in your organization. Set the standard. Live the standard. Lead the standard. In the immortal words of Populus Group CEO, Bobby Herrera, remember that, "Culture isn't something we're trying to create. Culture is the reason we exist."

It's come to that sacred time—the time for you to take what you've learned and apply it as you see fit. This is always the most exciting time for me because this is when I get emails and letters sharing how people's lives were impacted. I appreciate those more than you can imagine. I also get the emails and messages filled with suggestions about what could be different or better. I appreciate those as well. However, before you get fired up to send your notes off, pause to consider this.

You are the reason for the change you are seeing. It is because of you that your team is united. It is because of you that your customers are engaging more. Sit in that glow, even for just a moment. You earned it. You took action. You made the difference in the lives of those around you. If I played any part in that, it was only in helping you approach your people with the confidence to know that what you are doing is right.

If you'd like to share your stories, email ibelong@belongingfactor.com. I would appreciate nothing more than the gift of your time and your thoughts. Also, remember, because you purchased the book, you have unlimited access to the tools and resources available at book.belongingfactor.com. Check back regularly, as new and updated resources will be made available.

So now, it's your turn! Get out there and be a belonging champion, because you've got the Belonging Factor in you.

SET THE STANDARD

LIVE THE STANDARD

LEAD THE STANDARD

ACKNOWLEDGMENTS

This book was born from the idea that there is a better way. What started as in-depth philosophical discussions over a little too much wine and much laughter turned to journaled thoughts. Those journals became blog posts, which evolved into this messy, but amazing journey of writing *Belonging Factor*. It required more than I could have ever given it on my own.

First and foremost, thank you to my amazingly brilliant and beautiful wife, Kimberly, who always knows when to push me to the next step. You make me the best version of myself, and the gift of your unconditional love fuels me through the darkest nights.

To my parents, for dealing with my bullshit and loving me unconditionally. When I started this journey, you were supportive and proud. Mom, thank you for sticking with me through the tough times and growing with me. Dad, I wish you were here to see the final product of the love, support, and encouragement you always provided me. I miss you beyond words. Thank you for guiding and inspiring me to become the man I am today.

To my amazing boys, Cole and Cooper, who prove that biology is not a prerequisite for a loving family. I am so proud of you and the men you are becoming. Thank you for accepting me and challenging me to be the World's Greatest Dad!

To my editor and friend, Katrin Jesswein, who gave wholly and graciously. Thank you for driving me crazy with your quest for perfection and impeccable command of language. Both the book and I are better off because of it.

To Darren Webster, who took a chance on me, believed in me, and mentored me. I am proud to count you among my trusted friends. Thank you for never Americanizing your pronunciation of the word process (pr˙ō˙sess).

If someone ever tells you that writing a book is effortless, they haven't written a book. This process involved so many supportive, sometimes argumentative, intelligent, and committed people. To those whom I interviewed or bounced ideas off of, know that every moment was magical in this process. Lauren Aguilar, Jennifer Brown, Karen Catlin, Mike Ciprari, Andrea Flack-Wetherald, Paul Gedeon, Stephen Harroun, Bobby Herrera, Joanne Lockwood, Amy Lohr, Natalie Oliverio, Amy Perkins, Rhodes Perry, Alan

Schaefer, Crystal Swanson, Carolyn Swora, Karen Walker, Danny Willow. You are incredible people with incredible stories. Thank you for allowing me to share a small part of it with you.

Thank you to those who gave me the gift of time, brainpower, and encouragement. Without your feedback and support, this book would still be a mess of ideas lost in the ether.

Perhaps the most important group to thank is you. To those who give the gift of your time to read my ramblings, thank you. Thank you for the courage to take these ideas and put them into action. Thank you for embracing *Belonging Factor* and all that it calls you to be. Thank you for choosing to be the leader this world needs.

NOTES

10 *Psychologist Christopher Peterson...* Houston, Elaine. "Other People Matter: Christopher Peterson's Work in Positive Psychology." *PositivePsychology.com*, June 19, 2019. positivepsychology.com/christopher-peterson-other-people-matter/.

12 *Look at the numbers.* "The Business of BELONGING." The Analytics Maturity Model (IT Best Kept Secret Is Optimization). November 22, 2018. https://www.ibm.com/services/ibmix/brand-belonging/.

13 *We have a strong instinct...* Junger, Sebastian. *Tribe.* Fourth Estate Ltd, 2017.

15 *Not sold yet? Here are a few final numbers for you.* "The Business of BELONGING." The Analytics Maturity Model (IT Best Kept Secret Is Optimization). November 22, 2018. https://www.ibm.com/services/ibmix/brand-belonging/.

22 *Once we have formed a view...* Heshmat, Shahram, Ph.D. "What Is Confirmation Bias?" Psychology Today. April 23, 2015. https://www.psychologytoday.com/us/blog/science-choice/201504/what-is-confirmation-bias.

28 *While diversity is what...* McQuaid, Michelle. "Do Your People Feel Like They Belong?" *Psychology Today*, May 22, 2019. www.psychologytoday.com/us/blog/functioning-flourishing/201905/do-your-people-feel-they-belong.

39 *Great leaders are not born...* Sinek, Simon. *Leaders Eat Last.* Portfolio Penguin, 2018.

42 *Overcommunicate exactly how...* Herrera, Bobby. *The Gift of Struggle: Life-Changing Lessons About Leading.* Bard Press, 2019.

70 Photo courtesy of Lane Steel Company, Inc. © 2017

82 *We respond to every point of contact.* Halliday, Devin; Mike Ciprari. "*Belonging Factor* Podcast: An Interview with Mike Ciprari." April 28, 2019.

98 *If you truly want to understand...* Pellet, Liz. "Organizational Values." *SHRM*, SHRM, May 19, 2017. www.shrm.org/resourcesandtools/hr-topics/behavioral-competencies/global-and-cultural-effectiveness/pages/organizational-values.aspx.

99 *Operational objective are short term goals...* Zigu. "Operational Objectives Definition | Operations & Supply Chain Dictionary." *MBA Skool-Study.Learn.Share.* www.mbaskool.com/business-concepts/operations-logistics-supply-chain-terms/7317-operational-objectives.html.

106 *I go think back to when I was twelve years old.* Halliday, Devin; Mike Ciprari. "*Belonging Factor* Podcast: An Interview with Mike Ciprari." April 28, 2019.

NOW YOU CAN MAKE

BE/
LONG
/ING
FACTOR

A PART OF YOUR
ORGANIZATION OR TEAM

1. Take Your Learning Further by Listening to the *Belonging Factor* Podcast

2. Take Action & Introduce Belonging Factor Workshops to Your Organization

3. Make an Impact at Your Next Meeting or Team Function with Devin Halliday as Your Keynote Speaker

Take Your Learning Further by Listening to the *Belonging Factor* Podcast

The *Belonging Factor* podcast features content that expands the conversation involving all things belonging. Devin has interviewed some of the world's leading experts in diversity, inclusion, and belonging. Join the Belonging Factor family and subscribe to the podcast.

Available on all major podcast platforms, or listen on the web at podcast.belongingfactor.com.

Take Action & Introduce Belonging Factor Workshops to Your Organization

Belonging Factor half-day workshops are the perfect introduction for an organization interested in growing profits by transforming culture through a sense of belonging. Full-day workshops extend beyond introductions and provide the practical tools necessary to execute the fundamentals of the Belonging Factor.

Inquiries should be directed to ibelong@belongingfactor.com. For more information, visit www.belongingfactor.com.

Make an Impact at Your Next Meeting or Team Function with Devin Halliday as Your Keynote Speaker

Devin Halliday has been hailed as a dynamic and engaging speaker who "gets it." He speaks candidly, right to the heart and mind of his audiences. He has a way of immediately grabbing and holding an audience's attention, by saying things others are afraid to say, while simultaneously delivering measurable, actionable take-backs.

Inquiries should be directed to kim@belongingfactor.com, or visit www.devinhalliday.com.

ABOUT THE AUTHOR

Devin Halliday is an award-winning sales leader, with a diverse background and passion for people. He hosts the Belonging Factor Podcast, where he elevates the dialogue around diversity, inclusion and of course, belonging.

Devin is the Founder and Chief Belonging Architect at Rudiment Solutions, a people empowerment company that works with individuals and organizations to thrive in all things people, process and profits. Devin proudly served in the U.S. Navy.

Devin is a Northern California native. He's explored the people, places, and cultures across this beautiful planet. He's been amazed. He's been humbled. He's been outraged. But mostly, he's been inspired to share his lessons with audiences worldwide.